MY FIRST SCIENCE TEXTBOOK
Atoms

Los átomos

Written by Mary Wissinger
Illustrated by Harriet Kim Anh Rod

Created and edited by John J. Covey

Science, Naturally!
An imprint of Platypus Media, LLC
Washington, D.C.

T0002417

Say hello to the atoms that build everything you see:

Saluda a los átomos que construyen todo lo que ves:

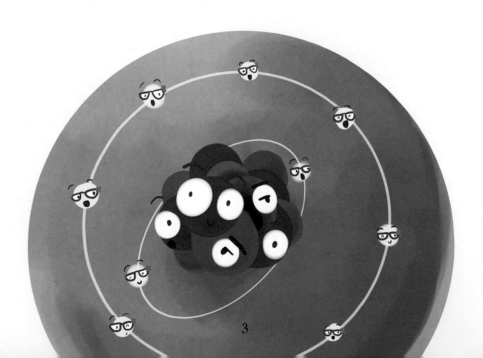

3

your hands, this book, the air,
giraffes, and every single tree.

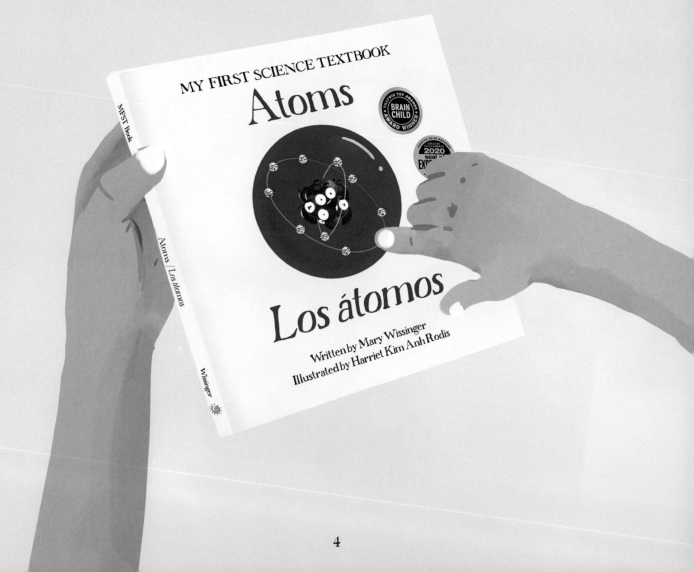

MY FIRST SCIENCE TEXTBOOK

Atoms

Los átomos

Written by Mary Wissinger
Illustrated by Harriet Kim Anh Rodis

Tus manos, este libro, el aire,
las jirafas y todos los árboles.

If you want to make an atom, the recipe starts with protons and neutrons.

Si quieres hacer un átomo, la receta empieza con protones y neutrones.

Squish them together, use high heat, and sprinkle in electrons.

Apretújalos bien, dales mucho calor y agrega al final los electrones.

The strong force holds the nucleus tight, while electrons get to race.

Una fuerza poderosa mantiene el núcleo apretado, mientras que los electrones dan vueltas alrededor.

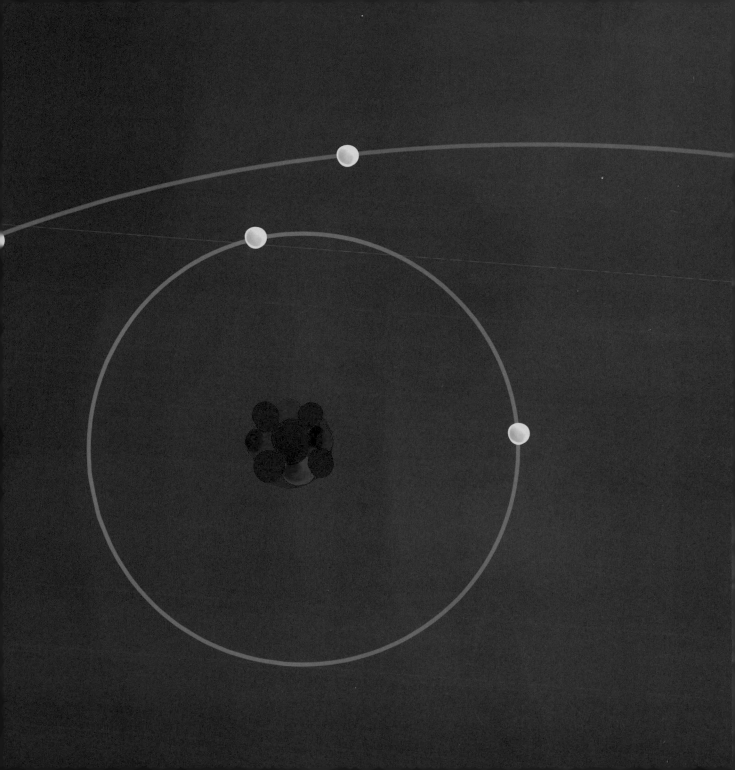

They fly so far from the nucleus that atoms are mostly empty space.

Viajan tan lejos del núcleo que se podría decir que el átomos está relleno de espacio vacío en su interior.

When atoms get together, electrons are for sharing and taking.

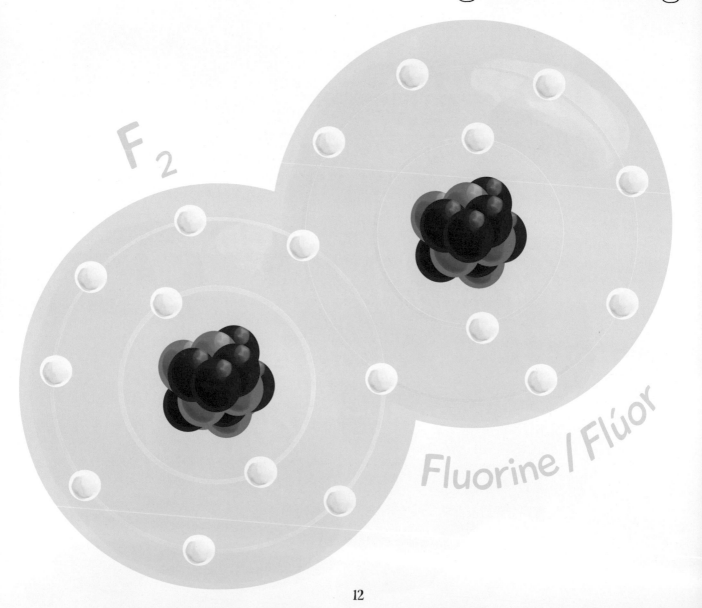

F_2

Fluorine / Flúor

Cuando los átomos se juntan, comparten electrones y los donan.

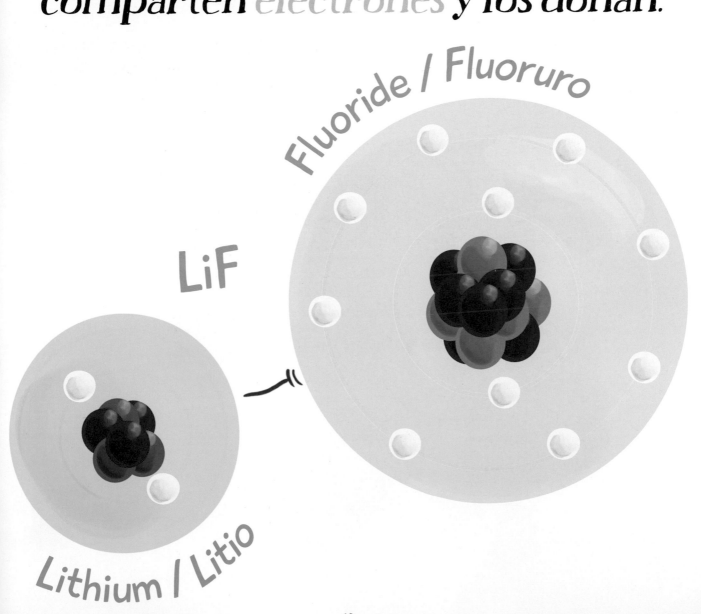

Fluoride / Fluoruro

LiF

Lithium / Litio

These covalent and ionic bonds are molecules in the making.

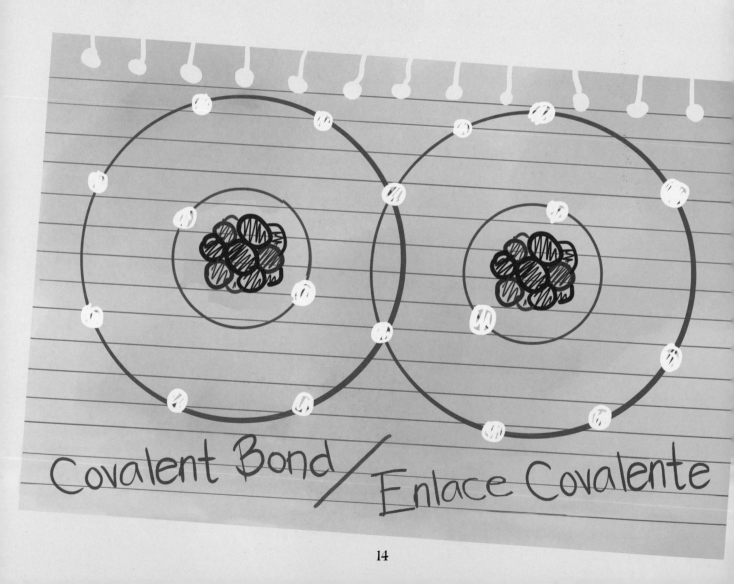

Covalent Bond / Enlace Covalente

Estos enlaces iónicos y covalentes son los que las *moléculas* forman.

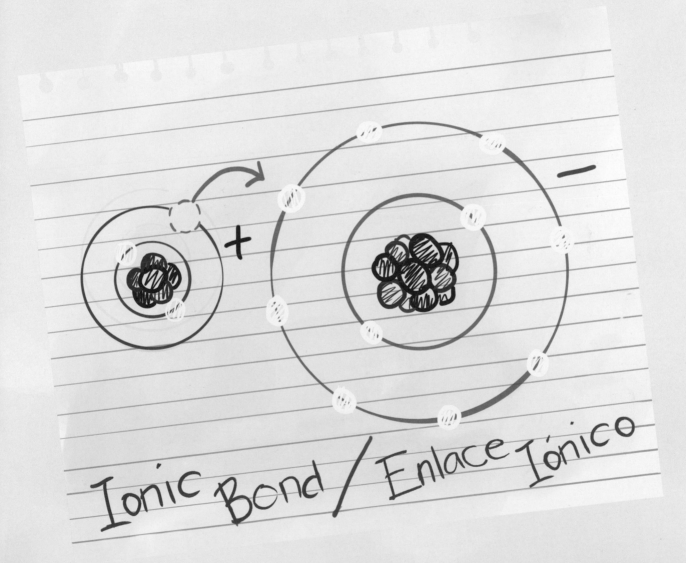

Ionic Bond / Enlace Iónico

There is a special word for when atoms look and act the same.

Existe una palabra especial para cuando los átomos lucen y actúan igual.

It's called an element,
and each element has a name.

Esa palabra es elemento, y cada elemento tiene un nombre individual.

Elements go in increasing order on the Periodic Table.

Los elementos en la tabla periódica están organizados en orden ascendente.

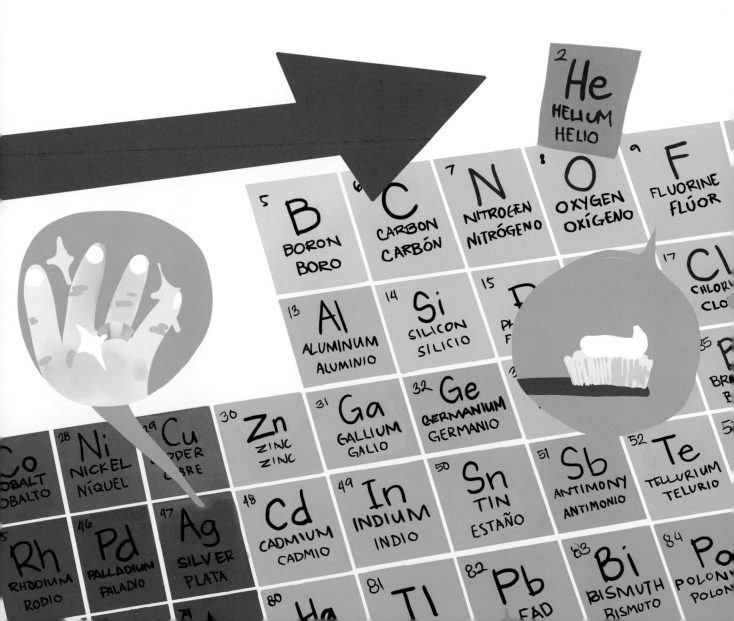

Atomic number, mass, chemical symbol...there are a lot of labels.

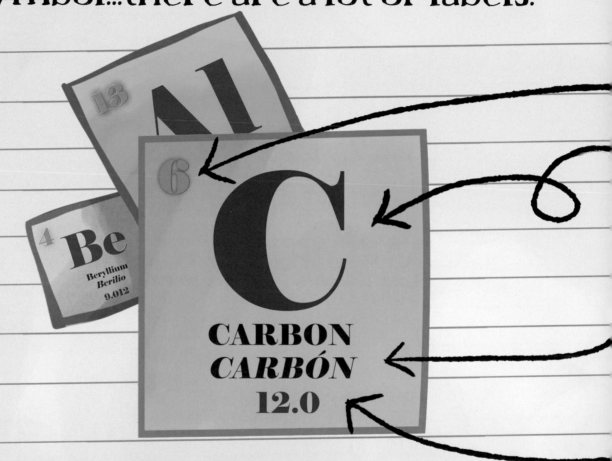

Número atómico, masa, símbolo... se pueden clasificar de muchas formas diferentes.

Atomic Number	Número Atómico
(the number of protons)	(la cantidad de los protones)
Chemical Symbol	Símbolo Químico
Name	Nombre
Atomic Mass	Masa Atómica
(the number of protons and neutrons)	(la cantidad de protones y neutrones)

These universal particles
are the same on Earth
as they are on Mars.

Estas partículas universales
son las mismas aquí en la
Tierra que en Marte.

Atoms compose each tiny speck
from here to distant stars.

*Los átomos componen cada puntito
diminuto desde aquí hasta la
estrella más distante.*

You contain galaxies of atoms, so protons, neutrons, and electrons, too.

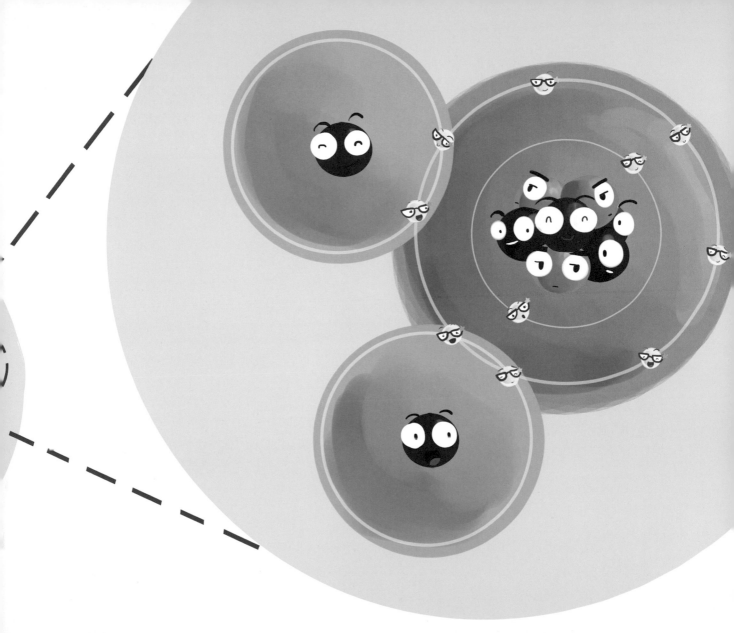

Hay galaxias de átomos, protones, neutrones y electrones dentro de ti.

You live in the universe,
and a universe lives in you.

Tú vives en el universo,
y un universo vive en ti.

Glossary

ATOMIC MASS: The combined number of protons and neutrons in an atom. On the periodic table, it is shown as the number under each element's full name.

ATOMIC NUMBER: The number of protons in an atom determines an element's atomic number, which is used to categorize elements. On the periodic table, the atomic number is shown in the top left-hand corner of each element label.

ATOMS: The building blocks for all matter in our universe. They are so small that you can't see them, and are made up of even smaller particles called protons, neutrons, and electrons.

CHEMICAL BONDS: Chemical bonds are what join atoms together to create molecules. There are several types of chemical bonds, including covalent and ionic bonds.

CHEMICAL SYMBOL: The abbreviation for the name of an element. The chemical symbol for each element is listed in the periodic table.

COVALENT BOND: A chemical bond that forms between two atoms when they share electrons.

ELECTRONS: Very teeny particles with a negative electric charge. Electrons travel around the nucleus of every atom.

ELEMENT: A pure substance made of one type of atom.

FORCE: The push or pull on something when it interacts with something else. A force can cause an object to move faster, slow down, stay in place, or change shape.

GALAXY: In astronomy, a galaxy is made up of billions of stars, which are each orbited by planets, gas, and dust. It can also mean a large group of people or things.

ION: An atom or molecule that carries a positive or negative electric charge as a result of having gained or lost electrons.

IONIC BOND: A chemical bond that forms when one atom gives away electrons to another atom. The atom that loses electrons becomes positively charged, and the atom that gains electrons becomes negatively charged.

MASS: A measure of how much matter is in an object. Mass is different from weight because the mass of an object never changes, but its weight will change based on its location in the universe.

MATTER: Matter makes up everything around you, and anything in the universe that takes up space and has mass.

MOLECULE: A group of atoms that are bonded together to form the smallest unit of a substance that has all the properties of that substance. For example, a water molecule is the smallest unit that is still water.

NEUTRONS: Very teeny particles with no electric charge, found in the nucleus of most atoms.

NUCLEUS: The center part of an atom, made up of protons and neutrons.

PARTICLES: Tiny, singular bits of matter that can range in size from subatomic particles, such as electrons, to ones large enough to be seen, such as particles of dust floating in sunlight.

PERIODIC TABLE: A chart that arranges chemical elements, organized by atomic number.

PROTONS: Very teeny particles with a positive electric charge. Protons are in the nucleus of every atom.

SUBATOMIC PARTICLE: A particle that is smaller than an atom and exists within it, like protons, neutrons, or electrons.

UNIVERSE: All of time and space and their contents, including planets and stars, and all other forms of matter and energy.

Glosario

ÁTOMOS: Son los bloques de construcción de toda la materia que existe en el universo. Son tan pequeños que no se pueden ver y están hechos de partículas más pequeñas llamadas protones, neutrones y electrones.

ELECTRONES: Partículas muy pequeñas con una carga eléctrica negativa. Los electrones viajan alrededor del núcleo de cada átomo.

ELEMENTO: Una sustancia formada por un solo tipo de átomo.

ENLACE COVALENTE: Un enlace químico que se forma en medio de dos átomos cuando ambos comparten electrones.

ENLACE IÓNICO: Un enlace químico que se forma cuando un átomo dona sus electrones a otro átomo. El átomo que pierde electrones se carga positivamente, y el átomo que gana electrones se carga negativamente.

ENLACES QUÍMICOS: Los enlaces químicos son aquellos que unen átomos para crear moléculas. Incluyen los enlaces iónicos y covalentes.

FUERZA: Toda acción que ejerce un objeto sobre otro. La fuerza puede causar que un objeto se mueva más rápido, más lento, se quede en el mismo lugar o cambie de forma.

GALAXIA: En astronomía, una galaxia está formada por billones de estrellas, alrededor de las cuales orbitan otros planetas, gases y polvo. También puede significar un grupo grande de personas o cosas.

ION: Un átomo o una molécula que lleva una carga positiva o una carga negativa como resultado de haber ganado o perdido electrones.

MASA: Es la medida de cuánta materia tiene un objeto. La masa es diferente del peso porque la masa de un objeto nunca cambia, pero el peso puede cambiar dependiendo en dónde esté el objeto en el espacio.

MASA ATÓMICA: La suma del número de neutrones y protones de un átomo. En la tabla periódica, suele estar debajo del nombre del elemento.

MATERIA: Forma todo que está a tu alrededor, y todo lo que en el universo ocupa espacio y tiene masa.

MOLÉCULA: Un grupo de átomos que se unen para formar la unidad más pequeña de una sustancia que tiene todas las propiedades de esa sustancia. Por ejemplo, una molécula de agua es la unidad más pequeña que puede considerarse agua.

NEUTRONES: Partículas muy pequeñas sin ninguna carga eléctrica, que se encuentran en el núcleo de casi todos los átomos.

NÚCLEO: El centro de un átomo, compuesto de protones y neutrones.

NÚMERO ATÓMICO: El número de protones en un átomo determina el número atómico del elemento, el cual se usa para categorizar el elemento. En la tabla periódica, el número atómico se muestra en la esquina superior izquierda de cada elemento.

PARTÍCULAS: Diminutos pedacitos de masa que pueden oscilar en tamaño desde partículas subatómicas, como los electrones, hasta partículas más grandes que se pueden ver a simple vista, como motas de polvo que se ven a la luz del sol.

PARTÍCULA SUBATÓMICA: Una partícula que es más pequeña que un átomo y existe dentro de él, como los protones, los neutrones y los electrones.

PROTONES: Partículas muy pequeñas con una carga eléctrica positiva. Los protones están en el núcleo de cada átomo.

SÍMBOLO QUÍMICO: Es la abreviación del nombre de un elemento. El símbolo químico de cada elemento aparece en la tabla periódica.

TABLA PERIÓDICA: Un cuadro que organiza los elementos químicos por número atómico.

UNIVERSO: Todo el tiempo y el espacio y lo que ellos contienen, incluyendo los planetas, las estrellas y todas las otras formas de materia y energía.

"For Honora, whose curiosity never stops inspiring me."
"Para Honora, cuya curiosidad nunca deja de inspirarme."

— John J. Coveyou, creator and editor

My First Science Textbook: Atoms / Los átomos
Copyright © 2021, 2020, 2016 Genius Games, LLC
Originally published by Genius Games, LLC in 2016

Written by Mary Wissinger
Illustrated by Harriet Kim Anh Rodis with Uzuri Designs
Created and edited by John J. Coveyou
Translated by Michelle A. Ramirez
Spanish-language consultants: Eida de la Vega and Lizabeth Paravisini-Gebert

Published by Science, Naturally!
Bilingual (En/Sp) paperback first edition • July 2021 • ISBN: 978-1-938492-39-6
Bilingual (En/Sp) eBook first edition • July 2021 • ISBN: 978-1-938492-40-2
English hardback first edition • 2016 • ISBN: 978-1-945779-02-2
    Second edition • November 2020
English paperback first edition • July 2021 • ISBN: 978-1-938492-41-9
English eBook first edition • 2016 • ISBN: 978-1-945779-08-4
English board book first edition • 2016 • ISBN: 978-1-945779-05-3

Enjoy all the titles in the series:
    Atoms • Los átomos
    Protons and Neutrons • Los protones y neutrones
    Electrons • Los electrones

Teacher's Guide available at the Educational Resources page of ScienceNaturally.com.

Published in the United States by:
    Science, Naturally!
        An imprint of Platypus Media, LLC
    725 8th Street, SE, Washington, D.C. 20003
    202-465-4798 • Fax: 202-558-2132
    Info@ScienceNaturally.com • ScienceNaturally.com

Distributed to the trade by:
    National Book Network (North America)
        301-459-3366 • Toll-free: 800-462-6420
        CustomerCare@NBNbooks.com • NBNbooks.com
    NBN international (worldwide)
        NBNi.Cservs@IngramContent.com • Distribution.NBNi.co.uk

Library of Congress Control Number: 2021931584

10 9 8 7 6 5 4 3 2 1

Printed in Canada